So...
You want to be a
Lawyer?

Victoria Hogg

KOGAN PAGE

Note: In this book, 'the profession' refers to the legal system of England and Wales. Scotland and Northern Ireland each have their own system.

<u>YOURS TO HAVE AND TO HOLD</u>
BUT NOT TO COPY

First published in 1999

Apart from any fair dealing for the purposes of research or private study, or criticism or review, as permitted under the Copyright, Designs and Patents Act 1988, this publication may only be reproduced, stored or transmitted, in any form or by any means, with the prior permission in writing of the publishers, or in the case of reprographic reproduction in accordance with the terms and licences issued by the CLA. Enquiries concerning reproduction outside these terms should be sent to the publishers at the undermentioned address:

Kogan Page Limited
120 Pentonville Road
London N1 9JN

© Victoria Hogg, 1999

The right of Victoria Hogg to be identified as the author of this work has been asserted by her in accordance with the Copyright, Designs and Patents Act 1988.

British Library Cataloguing in Publication Data

A CIP record for this book is available from the British Library.

ISBN 0 7494 2883 X

Typeset by Kogan Page
Printed and bound by Clays Ltd, St Ives plc

Contents

Acknowledgements	iv
Introduction	1
1 Getting started	4
2 The profession divides	12
3 Getting a foot in the door	22
4 Admission as a solicitor	32
5 Life at the Bar	41
6 Summary	47
Glossary	53
Want to know more?	56

Acknowledgements

Particular thanks to my parents for their unconditional support, M A Watkins for advice and encouragement over the years, Amanda Drane for her generous contribution and Danielle Johnson for nominating friends and colleagues to be interviewed.

Thank you to all those who shared their experiences of training with me: Sarah Bryant, Greg Dolan, James Fisher, Claire Fitzpatrick, Rachel Edwards, Pankaj Madan, Claire Oakes, Anna Quirke, Shilpen Savani, Tim Susulowsky, Louise Whaites and Laura Warne.

I am grateful to the Law Society for their information pack and to the Bar Council for assisting with general queries. In addition, I would like to thank Sue Phillips of Lincoln's Inn for the information she supplied.

Introduction

If you look the word 'lawyer' up in the dictionary, you will find it defined as 'a member of the legal profession'. Obvious? Well, not quite. A simple point that is often missed is that the term 'lawyer' covers the two branches of the legal profession. There are solicitors and barristers. Solicitors advise clients, draw up documents and conduct advocacy, mainly in the lower courts; barristers (the ones in the wigs) are specialist advocates, instructed by solicitors to act for clients, and working mainly in the higher courts.

Not everyone knows straight away that they want to be a lawyer. I was bitten by the bug when I was quite young. I found the work of the courts fascinating and I also liked the idea of a job where I would have to research points in order to find an answer. In the end, after doing some work experience, I choose to be a solicitor. Maybe you are still at school; or maybe you have had a different career up till now and feel the need for a change. Whatever your reasons, you will need to know the steps involved.

The idea of this book is to give you a feel for what it will be like during the years of training before you gain access to the legal profession. It is a slog, and definitely not for the faint-hearted, but it is a field of work that is keen to welcome new recruits. For a long time, lawyers have had a reputation for talking gobbledegook, and for charging huge fees seemingly for stating the obvious. In recent years, therefore, both sides of the profession have tried to modernize and get away from this public perception of its members. It is an uphill struggle, and its success is dependent upon fresh blood – students straight from school, or people who change career and join later in life – entering the profession and keeping the momentum going.

It is important to stress that the legal profession should not be viewed as exclusive. There is room – and a need – for a variety of people from different backgrounds. Although it used to be largely an all-male preserve, an increasing number of women have entered the profession recently, redressing the balance. The Law Society's Annual Statistical Report examines trends in the solicitors' profession; the 1997 figures showed that slightly more women than men were admitted to the Roll as solicitors. This is a continuing trend that started to show in 1992. At the Bar, the complaint was always that there were so few women judges, but the Bar Council has witnessed the same sort of trend as the Law Society; however, as judges are only appointed after many years' experience, this change in the balance will take a little longer to show through. Both the Law Society and the Bar Council are committed to policies of Equal Opportunities, and closely monitor the numbers of ethnic minority candidates joining the profession.

These days, access to training has been widened, so that it is offered by many more institutions and in a number of different forms. Most of the courses are now available part-time. I will not pretend that finding funding for training is easy; it certainly is not. Indeed, it is common for students to emerge from their studies to join the working world saddled with significant debts, which are only paid off after many years. In this book I will try to cover some possible sources of funding available.

The legal profession, in common with many others, has been hit by economic pressures in recent years. Again, there is an unfortunate public perception that you never see a poor lawyer. This simply is not true any more. The economic reality is that there is a huge demand for every job that is available. When you consider a career in law, you need to bear in mind the current situation. For those who want to become barristers, the Bar Council figures for 1997/8 show that only about half of the applicants for places on the Bar Vocational Course can be accepted, because of restrictions on the number of places available. Only half of those who undertake the course secure a pupillage and probably two-thirds of those secure a tenancy in the end. For solicitors, the situation is slightly better, but any improvement is slow to take effect. In 1997, just under three-quarters of those who sat the exams for the Legal Practice Course – the vocational stage of training to become a solicitor – passed. In 1996/7, the number of those registering training contracts, the apprenticeship stage of training for solicitors, actually increased compared with previous years. None the less, this still means that a significant number of people who wanted to become lawyers did not actually achieve their aim.

For both potential solicitors and barristers, the options for studying have been widened, leading to more available places. While this is excellent from the point of view of providing people with the opportunity to achieve the academic side of qualification, it does not, unfortunately, address the problem of the shortage of jobs. I don't want to be a messenger of doom, but it is only fair to spell out the difficulties, so that you may make decisions with your eyes open. Indeed, some of those who apparently 'fall by the wayside' in attempting to gain legal qualifications or employment, will, in fact, find a career that suits them better.

While I was interviewing people for this book, I was struck by the sheer tenacity and hard work that has been displayed by those who have made it. In some cases, it has taken many years to qualify and reach that goal, but they have stuck with it. Some of those I talked to found the exams hard going, but battled on, because they knew that they had what it takes to be a successful lawyer in practice. Almost everyone has had some sort of setback on the way, which they have had to overcome.

I am not able to give you a definitive guide. You will need to plan ahead and do your own research at each stage. This book should provide you with a 'flavour' of the profession from its inside. You will have to keep your eye on the next step and be prepared. As a lawyer you are likely to have an extremely rewarding career, provided you can cope with the hard work. It is not a career where you will ever be watching the clock in boredom; you are more likely to lament that there are not enough hours in the day!

There are many different careers available to a barrister or solicitor. Apart from time spent in court, there are opportunities in the public and private sector, commerce and industry. Many lawyers have gone on to achieve high-profile careers in public life, as politicians, media stars and even world leaders! They have used their training as a stepping stone to help them along the way. If you are really determined, the world is your oyster!

1

Getting started

Basic qualifications

You will need to have high grades at GCSE or the equivalent qualification. As in the construction of a building, it is vital to lay strong foundations. It is important to ensure you have traditional subjects such as English and Mathematics. A foreign language is always useful. This shows a broad academic base from day one.

The next step is A levels, or the equivalent qualification. The general consensus is that it is not a good idea to study Law at this level, as it is seen as 'dabbling'. This is not to say that people who have studied Law A level will not succeed, but it is wise to exercise caution. It would be worth checking this out with prospective colleges before choosing your subjects. Again, it is important to achieve good grades. You would be well advised to pick subjects that demonstrate an ability to write well. You are likely to have to write many essays for your degree if you read Law and, indeed, you will need excellent written skills in your career. Generally, 'traditional' subjects seem to be more acceptable, but this is not always the case.

Degree level

If you decide to read Law for your degree, check whether or not your chosen institution will award an LLB – a Bachelor of Laws – qualification. If you discover that your studies will lead to a BA (a Bachelor of Arts), or a BSc (a Bachelor of Science), then you may have to do some further studying after you graduate in order to cover all the required topics. These are known as the Seven Foundations of Legal

Knowledge. The obligatory modules are Contract, Tort, Equity and Trusts, Criminal, Property, Law of the European Union and Public Law. Further study may also be necessary if you choose to study Law with other subjects. (It is worth noting that some universities, including Oxford and Cambridge, award BAs in Law, but their courses do cover all the topics required.)

Places to read Law are hard-won. The institutions offering courses in Law can afford to ask for top grades. Go to visit colleges before applying, to give yourself a feel for what they are like. After all, you will be spending a few years studying there. You will impress them if you have undertaken work experience in a legal context (see p7).

Once you have got your Law degree, you will have achieved something that will always stand you in good stead, even if you decide ultimately not to pursue a legal career. It is widely known how difficult it is to gain a place to read Law, and it is the type of degree that is universally recognized and respected.

CPE or PGDL

> **Fact:** You don't need a Law degree to become a lawyer.

This fact may surprise you! You can read another subject for your degree and then convert to Law by studying for a further year afterwards. This is called the Common Professional Examination (CPE) or Postgraduate Diploma in Law (PGDL). (Graduates who have studied for a Law degree that did not cover all the topics required may also have to study for the CPE.)

If you choose to follow the CPE route, you will study the core topics of law – the Seven Foundations of Legal Knowledge – in a year. It is an action-packed experience, during which you will have to absorb your new subjects and sit exams in each. Those who have just spent three or four years studying for a degree may be used to the intensity, but others may find it more difficult.

One advantage of qualifying in this way is that you have another discipline. Having a background in another area, such as a science, may lead later to an interesting specialization in Law covering that field. In addition, if you decide in the end not to pursue a legal career, you will have another string to your bow. It is more important in the long term that you come out with a good class of degree. You are more likely to do this if you have picked a subject that particularly interests you. Study what you enjoy! For most of us, it is the only time when we can indulge in this sort of study.

The down side of this route is, of course, money. In order to study the CPE you will need to finance yourself for another year. There may be limited sources of funding from the local authority, depending on where you live, but most CPE students will find themselves on their own.

You can take the CPE at a variety of institutions. You will need to apply early, perhaps in January for the following September. I chose a new university (a former polytechnic), because the fees were reasonable and the pass rate was high. You will need to do your own research in advance. On passing I was also guaranteed a place for the next stage, which is the Legal Practice Course. You want to make sure you get through first time. It looks better to prospective employers and it will save you spending more time and money. The Colleges of Law at Chester, Guildford, London and York are the most traditional venues. Their fees are higher, but you might find that their facilities are more specialized. You will need to shop around to find an institution to suit your needs.

> **Tip:** One important piece of general advice, which also applies to Law undergraduates, is not to rush in and buy all the books on your book list before the course. Law textbooks are fiendishly expensive, and go out of date very quickly. Wait until you actually start the course before buying. The previous year's students are often happy to sell you some of the basic texts at a knock-down price, and you will be able to do the same for the year below, once you have completed your studies.

Whether you have read Law, or another subject, it is vital that you come out with a good class of degree. You should aim for at least a second, or higher. Candidates with other classes of degree have made it but, in the light of current competition for places, it will help if you can show a good performance at this level. Some firms and sets of chambers will not consider people who have achieved less than an upper second class degree.

Once you have completed this stage of studying, you will be ready for the final year of exams (see the next chapter).

ILEX

> **Fact:** It is possible to qualify as a solicitor without obtaining a degree.

The non-graduate route is only available to potential solicitors at present. It involves becoming a solicitor via the Institute of Legal Executives (ILEX). It takes a long time, but it means that you can 'earn as you learn'. It is particularly valuable to mature students (those over 25 years of age), who may not have any formal qualifications. They may be able to put forward their experience of work and life instead. The details of this route are beyond the scope of this book, but the above fact confirms that the legal profession is not as exclusive as it may at first seem.

Getting your feet wet

I found it enormously helpful to do unpaid work in various areas of the profession while I was studying. This not only looks good on your CV, but may also help you to choose which areas interest you. After doing some work experience, I decided that I would become a solicitor rather than a barrister.

One of my first placements allowed me to shadow a barrister at the Crown Court when I left school. I sat in court and observed the proceedings. My next placement was organized by my Sixth Form College as an end-of-term project. At the time, I was bitterly disappointed not to be allocated work in a 'real' solicitor's office, as I saw it. Instead, I was posted to the local magistrates' court. I shadowed the Clerk to the Justices, the chief legal advisor. I was able to observe many different types of court, including Adult Criminal, Liquor Licensing and Private Prosecutions, where organizations such as the

Environment Agency bring cases. I was given some research to do to help me familiarize myself with certain legal manuals used by the legal team. I even acted as an usher for a morning, taking the names of those attending and calling them in when their case was on. I was taken to the various courthouses in the area, covered by that legal division. I had a fantastic time and, later, the experience led to me starting my career in the Magistrates' Court Service.

> **Tip:** Always turn up for work experience dressed as for court, for example, in a dark-coloured suit. If you look like a professional, you will show that you are serious and you may be introduced to more people than if you are casually dressed. I, myself, have been too embarrassed to introduce inappropriately dressed work-experience trainees to colleagues. They are creating the wrong impression, and are, therefore, wasting a golden opportunity to make useful contacts.

You don't need to have contacts to get work experience. Amanda had no contacts, but undertook a wide variety of placements as a result of her own initiative. She recommends writing early, for example, in January for a summer placement. When she was 16 years old, Amanda did a two-week placement with the Crown Prosecution Service (CPS). She returned to them during the summer holidays of the same year. This shows how one placement can lead on to another. She suggests visiting the local magistrates' court and observing. Once you are 14 years old you are allowed into a court. By talking to the ushers you can find out where the best cases are. Some of the courts, such as youth courts, are closed to the public, but the ushers will be able to tell you which ones you can go into. Ushers normally wear black gowns, and carry clipboards, so they are easily recognized! Most courts have a reception area where you can introduce yourself and say what you are interested in.

Amanda managed to secure paid work for two summers at her local magistrates' court. As she had a clear ambition to go to the Bar, she did some mini-pupillages (similar to the one that I did), during which she shadowed barristers at court. She used a guide called *The Chambers and Pupillages Award Handbook*, which she obtained through the Bar

Council. Aspiring lawyers can look up chambers and write to them, sending a copy of their CV and stating what stage they have reached. One drawback to be aware of is the cost of travelling to placements; if possible, look for more local experience as an alternative.

Pankaj warns against doing too many mini-pupillages. It may be better to do fewer and to do them well, rather than to go for blanket coverage and spread yourself too thinly. This could spoil your chances later on.

If you are very lucky, you may be able to marshal – sit with a Judge or Recorder at the Crown Court. Marshalling is an impressive placement! It may be possible to arrange this sort of experience if you are shadowing a senior barrister, but it is probably better to wait to be invited. It is perhaps the one instance when pushiness will not gain results! Later on, if you decide to pursue a career at the Bar, this sort of placement may be available through the Inns of Court (see Chapter 5).

It will not always be very exciting. Lawyers are busy people and they may not always have the time to think up interesting projects for you to do. You may spend a lot of time on the photocopier or filing. At least you will get an idea of what the profession is all about. If you can do the mundane stuff graciously, you may well be rewarded with something more to get your teeth into.

Work experience is a great way of establishing contacts, which can be useful later. If you make a good impression, you may be able to ask for advice or references (see 'Finding a mentor', p11).

The best way to obtain work experience, if you do not have particular contacts, is to write to as many places as you can. Apply early, and ensure you are persistent, because there is fierce competition, particularly for placements in the more prestigious firms or sets of barristers. I found the *Chambers and Partners Directory of the Legal Profession*, published every year, extremely useful as a source not only of names and addresses, but also of statistics about the profession in general. I obtained my copy through a law fair, but school careers departments or libraries may have a copy. Other useful directories are *The Legal 500* by John Pritchard, and the *Solicitors' and Barristers' National Directory* and *Regional Directory*, both published by the Law Society.

When you come to apply for your degree place, or later, when you are doing final exams, you should be able to demonstrate a real commitment to joining the profession. However, circumstances may mean that it is not always possible to show such commitment. Sarah changed careers after three years as an accountant. She had no work experience and her local careers service rather unhelpfully told her she was too old to do any of the placements they had. Greg also changed careers from Accountancy to Law. He continued working until he could pay for his exams, so there was no time to fit in work experience before he started studying, but he was able to obtain work experience later by writing off to firms.

Work experience may put you off the legal profession altogether, and is perhaps the best way of finding out if a career in Law is for you. It may save you spending years on a dream which, in reality, is not what you want. A work placement may also help you to make sense of some of the subjects you are studying, to see how the academic side translates into reality. If you are reading for a Law degree or, later on, studying for one of the sets of exams, there is nothing like the real thing to help you to get to grips with it all. During my final year of exams, we were told to go up to our local magistrates' court on a Saturday morning to see applications for bail being presented. This gave us a feel for what would be required when we came to present them ourselves.

Pankaj was undecided about whether to train as a barrister or solicitor. As in my case, work experience helped him to decide. Initially, he did a work placement with a local firm of solicitors with whom he had a connection. He got the opportunity to go up to his local Crown Court during the placement and found that he was fascinated by the court business. Later on, he managed to secure two placements – both paid – at large law firms. When, on one occasion, he went to brief counsel with one of the solicitors, he decided that he wanted to be on the other side of the table, being briefed! At university, Pankaj found that many students were being persuaded away from a career at the Bar because of the current job situation. After doing a broad range of work experience on both sides, he knew that he definitely wanted to go to the Bar, and he was able to make an informed decision about his future.

Finding a mentor

Finding a mentor need not be as formal as it sounds. In most professions, trainees will find someone to inspire and advise them. In my case, the Clerk to the Justices whom I met while on work experience from the sixth form gave me invaluable guidance when I was struggling to find a Training Contract. He suggested places for me to apply to and gave me the impetus to do it. When I did get a position, he advised me what I needed to achieve during my first couple of years.

A mentor may be a friend of your family, a teacher, or someone who is actually working in the profession. When you meet someone who you feel could help, keep in touch. Fill them in on your progress every so often. Remember that they are likely to be very busy, so do not badger them!

A mentor cannot do the job for you, but he or she can steer you in the right direction, and can give you more inside information than a careers department, for example. The careers officer at my college did not know which journals advertised the kinds of jobs that I was interested in. Generally speaking, they have to provide advice on a broad range of careers and, therefore, do not have the necessary specialist expertise. I had not realized that I could do a Training Contract in the magistrates' court, and had incorrectly assumed that you had to be qualified before you could enter that side of the profession. The advice of my 'mentor' was invaluable.

Others have had similar experiences. Danielle met a local solicitor who was a friend of the family. She did work experience for him for several summers and was able to return to him for advice when she was qualifying. Laura was able to secure a Training Contract and a full-time position with the solicitor with whom she had done work experience. When applying for and picking a pupillage, Pankaj turned to people whom he had met while studying for advice.

Once you have graduated or converted your degree, you have laid the ground work and reached the time for the final year of exams. You will have to decide whether to go to the Bar as a barrister, or to qualify as a solicitor. Read on…

2

The profession divides

When you come to your final year of study, you need to make a choice – to become a barrister or solicitor. This determines which final year of study you undertake.

Barrister or solicitor – what are the differences?

- Barristers specialize in advocacy – that is, in simple terms, arguing a case in court.
- Barristers provide a legal opinion for solicitors when asked to consider a particular question of law.
- Barristers are never instructed directly by clients, but always by solicitors on behalf of clients.
- Barristers are usually self-employed.
- Barristers work in co-operative groups called sets of chambers.
- Barristers are governed by a professional body called the Bar Council.
- Barristers are called to the Bar by the Inns of Court, which they must join.
- Barristers wear wigs and gowns in the County Court, Crown Court and higher courts.
- Barristers automatically have rights of audience in the higher courts.

Most barristers are self-employed. This attracted Amanda, who liked the idea of being able to take time out if she wished. Louise did not want to work for someone else, and liked the idea of a job that involved speaking in a formal setting. Pankaj was fascinated by the work of a barrister in court – the formalities, the traditions and the 'theatre' of the job. The aspiring barrister has to enjoy being on his or her feet, arguing cases in court most of the time, and needs to feel confident in that sort of setting.

- Solicitors are instructed directly by clients and have a great deal of contact with those clients.
- Solicitors carry out a mixture of work, including preparing and drafting documents, advising clients and representing them in court.
- Solicitors have rights of audience in the lower courts, that is, in the Magistrates' Court and the County Court.
- Solicitors can gain rights of audience in the higher courts with further training.
- Solicitors do not wear wigs, although they do wear gowns if they are appearing in the County Court or have higher rights of audience.
- Solicitors are largely employed in private practice, being based in offices.
- Solicitors instruct barristers on behalf of clients.
- Solicitors are governed by a professional body called the Law Society.

I enjoyed the research side of the profession, but wanted more contact with clients, so I chose to be a solicitor. I did not want the financial uncertainty of being self-employed. Some barristers are employed, but terms of employment will probably not be your first consideration when looking at which branch to join. You should look instead at what sort of working life you think you will enjoy. If you have done some work experience, then you will have some idea by this time. Clearly, you need to make the decision at an early stage, so that you can apply to institutions in plenty of time. If you want to be a solicitor, you will study the Legal Practice Course. If you want to be a barrister, you will go to Bar School.

Legal Practice Course (LPC)

This year used to be known as Law Society Finals, and was completely exam-based. However, it was felt that this did not prepare students for the practical realities of being a solicitor. The whole year depended on success in end-of-year exams. The new course is designed to provide the student with the skills required for the job. There are exams throughout the year, and ultimate success depends upon a consistent performance, rather than one big push at the end. The course is also designed to develop and test certain practical skills, which the trainee solicitor will need in his or her working life.

You can study the LPC at a wide range of places, either full-time (one year) or part-time (two years). The Law Society produces a list of those institutions validated for the course. You can choose between the traditional Colleges of Law at Chester, Guildford, London and York, and a variety of universities and institutes. Some of these provide the course in joint venture with another. You will need to apply early in the preceding year, that is, during the spring of your final year of Law degree or CPE. Forms are available from the LPC Central Applications Board at Guildford in the autumn. You will need to have enrolled as a student member of the Law Society and have a Certificate of Completion of the academic stage before you can be accepted on the course. This can take some time, while references relating to your suitability to be a solicitor are checked. You should also become a student member of the Trainee Solicitors Group (TSG). This group fights for the rights of its members on a variety of issues, including minimum salaries while training.

I found that the college where I studied the CPE guaranteed a place on the LPC to all those who passed. If you plan to come by the same route as I did, check whether your own institution does this or not. The cost of the course will vary from place to place. (For more details on costs, and possible methods of funding see chapter 6.)

What is involved?

Certain subjects are compulsory: Business Law and Practice, Litigation and Advocacy, Conveyancing, Wills, Probate and Administration and Accounts. You will sit exams in these subjects. In the first term, if you are studying the full-time course, you will do some of the subjects and then sit the exams relevant to those at the end of the term. This way, you are not required to undertake a big memory test at the end of the year, and you can really focus on the subjects in hand. In addition, you will have to study two optional subjects from a range on offer; these will vary according to the institution where you are studying, and will cover topics in 'private client' and 'corporate client' work.

While you are studying the theory in these compulsory areas, you will also be learning the skills that will help you to apply them. These include Practical Legal Research, Drafting and Writing, Interviewing and Advising, Negotiating and Advocacy. In addition, you will be instructed on matters of Professional Conduct, including, for example, identifying a conflict of interest between yourself and a client whom you are representing. You will also see how the Financial Services Act 1986 applies in relation to Investment Business. This can be relevant in a range of situations when dealing with clients on other matters. You will learn when you can give certain financial advice to clients and when you need some authorization by a professional body. These two areas are known as Pervasive Topics because they regularly feature in the study of the compulsory subjects.

What is it really like?

When I studied the LPC, it was the first year of the newly designed course. It was really a test year to see how it would all work. Perhaps the most notable difference was the practical aspect. Previously, students had been required to learn factual subjects, suddenly we were having to apply that knowledge and think on our feet, just as we would have to in real life. In Business Law, we set up a mock company and learned the basics by applying them to 'the company' at each stage. In Wills and Probate, we were videoed advising a client on the provisions of a relative's will. For the Advocacy skill, we had to present application for bail and a plea in mitigation. This was a practical application of our criminal litigation theory. These practicals were nerve-wracking. In order to feel the part, we were asked to dress for court, and the fact that we were also being videoed only served to heighten the tension!

For the Negotiating skill, we were split into pairs and asked to conduct a negotiated settlement on damages. What actually happened was probably not what had been intended. As soon as we found out who our opposite numbers were, we sought them out, and began to work out how to conduct the exercise. In this way, the actual negotiation was done before the video started running!

These practical exercises proved to be valuable experiences. It is far better to mess up a practice session than to fail when you have a real client relying on you. Although it is hard to believe it at the time, it is beneficial. You enter the profession, when you start work on your Training Contract, having had a go. This gives you some much-needed confidence. Of course, it takes many years to hone the skills to perfection, but at least you have an idea of what you should be doing.

You will find that people take the course very seriously and this can add to the pressure. This is often because a significant amount of money has been paid out for fees, and students want to make sure not only that they complete the course successfully, but also that they achieve the best results they can. I found the atmosphere very different to that on previous courses. You are expected to study in a professional way. Missing lectures is certainly not acceptable. At the college I attended, we were told that if we missed any sessions we would be off the course.

Greg was one student who felt there were some flaws with the LPC. He had found the CPE challenging but thought that the LPC did not, in fact, prepare students for doing the job. Some of the exams are 'open book', which means you can take your notes in. The idea behind this is that in real life you will not be expected to know everything by heart, and will always have an opportunity to look points up. The course sets out to develop the skill of knowing where to look to find the answer. Greg felt that this system led to a tendency to rely too heavily on notes, without actually learning essential information. In his opinion, this meant that, if a real client's problem was not in your notes, then you were stumped.

Bar School

This stage of a lawyer's education has also undergone a number of changes very recently. Previously, if you wanted to be a barrister, you had to go to the Inns of Court School of Law in London to study.

Now the Bar Vocational Course (BVC) is available at selected institutions that have been validated to run the course. These are at Newcastle, Nottingham, Bristol, Cardiff and Manchester, as well as London.

According to Louise, the decision of which institution to attend requires careful thought, as most chambers are based in London. If you particularly want to practise in a certain part of the country, it would make sense to go to the nearest place for your BVC. If, however, you are undecided on where to practise, it might be better to opt for London; that way, you will have less travelling for interviews when applying for pupillages, which is the next step. Pankaj's view is that London is the best place to develop a feel for the Bar and its traditions and values. It would be harder outside London, he thinks, to foster a sense of what the profession of a barrister is all about. He accepts, however, that in some cases finances might dictate the choice, with living expenses being so high in London.

The BVC can be done on a full-time or part-time basis, and it runs for one or two years respectively. It is designed to prepare the student for the pupillage stage by providing him or her with the skills and knowledge of evidence and procedure that they will need to make the most of their training.

How do I apply?

There is a centralized clearing system known as CACH (Centralized Applications and Clearing House). You need to apply either in the autumn term of your final year of your degree, if you are reading Law, or in the first term of the CPE if you have done another degree. You are allowed to apply for three courses, specifying your order of preference. If you are unsuccessful with these, you can opt to go in for clearing at a later stage.

Joining an Inn

A prerequisite for being accepted on the BVC is that you should be a member of one of the Inns of Court. These are really societies for barristers. There are four Inns: Gray's Inn, Inner Temple, Lincoln's

Inn and Middle Temple. They all have long histories and particular traditions. Gray's Inn, for example, dates back to before the reign of Elizabeth I. During her reign, the Inn was popular among those at her court. William Shakespeare is reputed to have acted in the Hall at the Inn. Charles Dickens used the Inn in two of his novels, *David Copperfield* and *The Pickwick Papers*. The overall running of the Inns is governed by the Masters of the Bench. These are very senior members of the profession including judges and Queen's Counsel. They are sometimes called Benchers. Their collective formal meetings are known as Pension. The Masters are responsible for the Call to the Bar. 'Being called' is the expression used for the process of qualifying to be in a position to practise either as an independent advocate in England and Wales or in employment as a barrister.

The Inns have facilities such as libraries and dining rooms. Some students join at an earlier stage, so that they can use the library. The date on which you join affects the order in which you are called. If you join early, you will be one of the first called. Only the Inns have the power to call a person to the Bar of England and Wales.

Amanda went along to a garden party at her future Inn, and she was able to build up a connection that led to her choice. Louise chose her Inn because it had an established northern tradition with a number of prestigious northern practitioners as members. She also liked the fact that it was located near to where she was studying, and this meant that the library was near by. Pankaj chose his Inn because it had close links with his college.

Your choice of Inn may be affected by the number of scholarships available. In some cases, an entrance award is offered, which covers all your basics costs upon entrance, from your entrance fee to your dinners (see p 20). There may be other bursaries available to cover the costs of your fees at Bar School. Some universities, as Pankaj found, have close links with particular Inns. The Inns have open days, on which you can be shown around. The best advice seems to be to write to each of the Inns, see what they are offering, and then make your choice.

What will I study on the BVC?

The main legal subjects are Evidence, Civil Litigation, Criminal

Litigation and Sentencing. In addition, you can choose two optional subjects from a selection of six. These are tested largely by means of multiple choice.

On the skills side, many areas are covered, in order to set you up for your working life at the Bar. These are divided into areas. The first group includes Case Work skills, Fact Management and Legal Research. The second focuses on Writing, both from a general point of view, and in specialist form; this might involve study of Opinion Writing, which is when a lawyer provides written legal advice, and Drafting, or the production of various documents. These subjects are all likely to be tested in written papers.

The last group of skills to be covered centres on the person – Interpersonal skills and Conference skills. A conference is the term used to describe a meeting with a client and instructing solicitor. Negotiation and Advocacy are also studied. These are likely to be tested by way of practical exercises, some of which will be videoed.

What is it really like?

Amanda found the legal subjects were taught in a very academic way, and that she was required to memorize great chunks of information. She did not particularly rate the multiple choice method of testing knowledge, commenting that the specimen answers often did not fully cover the questions. She found that brushing up on Contract and Tort and Damages before the Negotiation skills test was very helpful.

Louise found the practical side much more enjoyable than the theory. She had already decided which area of practice she wanted to pursue, and consequently had to put up with being taught things she knew she would not need.

Pankaj got involved in social activities and became the Moots Officer for the Committee of his Inn when he was at Bar School. Mooting, rather like debating, is the discussion of a hypothetical legal case, sometimes undertaken in a formal setting. He entered various prestigious competitions, ultimately having to moot in front of some of the most distinguished judges in the country, and an audience of over one hundred. This proved to be a valuable experience. Not only did it help in building his confidence, and in encouraging him to think on his feet, but it also meant that Pankaj got to know a lot of people at his Inn.

Dinners

> **Fact:** In order to be called to the Bar, you have to eat a number of dinners.

This may sound peculiar to an outsider! In order to be called by one of the Inns, a student must complete twelve qualifying units. This is where the tradition of dining comes in. In the old days, the idea was that a student mixed with senior members of the profession and learned from them by dining with them. Amanda felt, however, that students at this stage tended to eat their dinner and rush out as quickly as was decently possible!

These days, units may be obtained in a number of ways. You might choose to attend a weekend session either at the Inn or at a residential centre. Some of the Inns have contacts with a beautiful country house on the Royal Estate at Windsor, which is used for educational purposes. A weekend session normally counts as three qualifying units. This is very helpful to those students who are outside London in terms of maximizing any visits and travelling costs. Also available are Education Days, which, again, may suit students who are outside London. You can fit in several units during one day. There are also Education Dinners, where you have dinner and a lecture, Domus Dinners, where students and seniors are together, and Social Dinners.

Dining takes place in terms, rather like terms at school. These are Hilary (January/February), Easter (May), Trinity (July), and Michaelmas (November). During the dinners, special toasts and customs are sometimes observed.

The variety of opportunities for gaining qualifying units avoids a situation in which students take part in dining simply so they can be called, without really benefiting from it. The different sessions, days out and dinners offer the perfect opportunity to mix and to meet people.

Pankaj particularly enjoyed dining in. He found it a pleasure to dine with friends and colleagues rather than an obligation. He felt that the bond between members, which was fostered by dining together in the Inns, was a very important part of the tradition of the Bar. In his view, being barrister is more than just a job. In order to understand the values of the profession, and uphold them, it is important to become involved in the traditions, and that includes dining.

Being called to the Bar

Once you have completed the requisite number of units, including dining, you will be in a position to be called. The order in which you are called depends on when you joined the Inn. There is an opportunity for friends and family to attend a ceremony. It is a tremendous achievement to join such a distinguished profession.

And finally...

It is worth noting that the University of Northumbria is the one provider of Exempting Law Degrees, which incorporate the academic and the vocational stages of training for barristers and solicitors in a four-year course. Other institutions may offer this course in the future.

3

Getting a foot in the door

The next stage is a difficult one. You have completed the main academic stages on your way to being a barrister or solicitor. It is now time to put that training into practice, and undertake your apprenticeship.

> **Fact:** It takes one year less to qualify as a barrister than it takes to qualify as a solicitor.

You may be surprised to learn that, while a solicitor's training takes two years, a barrister's training takes only one. There is a good deal of professional rivalry between the two branches of the profession, and I am sure representatives of each would be able to put forward plenty of theories for this, not all of them favourable! Perhaps a more straightforward explanation is that the nature of each job is very different, and therefore the type of training required is different. A barrister is a specialist focusing on court work, whereas the work of the solicitor covers a wide range, and he or she therefore needs broader skills.

Training Contracts

The Training Contract, formerly known as 'Articles of Clerkship' or 'Articles', takes two years to complete. After all your education, it is at last a chance to show what you are made of! During the period of the Training Contract, you will have to cover both contentious work, such as Family or Criminal where there is likely to be some litigation and non-contentious work, such as conveyancing, and be able to demonstrate an ability to apply the skills that you have acquired during your academic training. During your contract you will need to cover at least three different legal topics, such as Family, Criminal and Conveyancing. You will be required to keep a record of your training.

Danielle felt there was a big step up from postgraduate training courses to the Training Contract. She had come across some very capable lawyers who, although they had found the exams a struggle, really came into their own once they were dealing with real people. On the other hand, she knew some brilliantly academic people who did not have the first idea about handling clients. She felt the tests along the way did not necessarily give a very good indication of how good each student could be as a solicitor. The message here is to stick with it, if you know you have got what it takes.

As a trainee solicitor you will find yourself involved in all aspects of the job. Danielle found that she had to keep to time targets and financial targets, even though she was not expected to bring clients to the firm. You might also be expected do marketing or PR for the firm. She commented that these are subjects in which students do not receive training.

If you want to work in the courts doing criminal or civil work, the opportunities for getting experience 'on your feet' are limited. You will not obtain full rights of audience until you qualify. You can, however, make applications in chambers before District Judges. My job in the Magistrates' Court Service was unusual in that I was able to clerk courts before I qualified. As a result, I was having to make decisions on points of law, and manage the court list, gaining experience as I went along. It was daunting at first but, like anything else, I got used to it. I found that this helped me enormously when it came to the Advocacy module in the Professional Skills Course (PSC). I was used to addressing the court, and to hearing the sound of my own voice!

Other people find the scope of their Training Contract more limited, because the business of the firm may be too important to let a trainee loose on it. This meant the trainee had to carry out more menial tasks, and thus felt less well prepared at the end of the contract for the transition from trainee to qualified solicitor.

How do I get a Training Contract?

Getting a contract is not an easy task. There are limited places and many students. Remember that the other students will also have the necessary qualifications. This is when it pays to have picked your subjects and your university carefully. You will need to be able to market yourself in such a way that you have an edge over your competitors. Think about what points on your CV are going to make you stand out. Work experience will be invaluable at this stage.

There is no right or wrong way to go about finding a contract. Several directories are published each year covering most, if not all, of the firms in the country and listing what areas of practice they cover (see Chapter 1, about work experience). You will also find them listed in the 'Want to know more?' section at the end of this book. There are often other useful statistics in the directories, such as how many trainees each firm usually recruits. These publications are likely to be available in your local careers service. You should not, however, use them as a substitute for your own research. If you have a particular interest, do not apply to a firm that does not cover your area just because you have failed to check which areas it does cover. You may find that some of the larger firms use their work experience programmes as a means of finding candidates for Training Contracts. Of course, this does not guarantee you the job, but it can only help you if they know what your work is like.

When do I apply?

The Law Society suggests that you apply during your final term if you are reading Law, and in the autumn term if you are studying for the CPE. Some students find that they finish their postgraduate training and still do not have a Training Contract. In my year, this was a big percentage of the class. It may be a good idea to have something lined up as a fall-back option to tide you over until you acquire a contract. If this work is of a legal nature, it may count towards your contract in the end. (See the end of this chapter for some of the options available.)

I found that I was getting nowhere by sending speculative applications to firms. I went to ask for advice from the Justices Clerk with whom I had done work experience. He pointed me towards the *Justice of the Peace Journal*, in which the Magistrates' Courts jobs were advertised. I had not realized that I could do a Training Contract in that way. I had always thought that I would need to qualify first, and then specialize in the Courts Service. As the *Journal* is not widely available in careers services, he arranged for me to leave some self-addressed envelopes at his office, so that every time there was a job I received notice of it. Within about three weeks I had got my Training Contract! My success was down to focusing my search.

Greg found his Training Contract when a friend was offered one by a firm for whom he had done work experience. The friend had already got a place with another firm, so he invited Greg to write to them instead. Generally, however, you will have to look for the openings yourself. No one will do it for you! Greg was surprised that other students on his course were seemingly so unmotivated. He felt some of them had been on a treadmill because they had read for a Law degree. Qualifying as a solicitor was seen by them simply as the next step. However, no student will automatically acquire a contract because he or she has done the exams.

In James's opinion, you should not overlook applying locally for a Training Contract. After his degree he did four weeks' work experience at a local firm. He treated it like a job and got a lot out of his placement. As he had done a Business Law degree, the firm wanted to know why he was not applying for jobs in the City. He said that he saw no harm in working elsewhere, and that he had not found City work particularly enjoyable anyway. The local connection gave him an introduction because they knew the schools he had been to.

Claire is in a general practice in her local area. She made use of local contacts in order to secure her Training Contract. In fact, she received three offers, and was then able to choose the one that suited her best.

Will I get paid?

You may hear senior solicitors refer to the fact that in the past they actually paid an employer in order to undertake Articles with them. Now, the employer pays you a salary to work as a trainee for them. At present there is a Law Society agreed minimum salary for trainees, and you would generally not expect to work for less than this.

However, some firms have found ways of paying less than the minimum; some take trainees on in a paralegal capacity, expecting them to undertake all manner of tasks, many of a legal nature. In this situation, the trainee is generally not offered a Training Contract, but is promised that they will be offered one if they shape up well. The trainee may ask for this work to be credited towards the two-year training period.

Firms are able to find ways around the Law Society minimum pay because of the demand for Training Contracts. Some trainees take the view that, as long as they can qualify, they will put up with a certain amount of hardship in the mean time. One major difficulty with this is that you are still expected to live the lifestyle and look the part, and this costs money. You may be very short of funds, if you are paying back loans and are not being paid even the minimum salary. The Trainee Solicitors Group, a national organization which you will hear about when you join the Law Society as a trainee member, fights hard for these basic rights.

Professional Skills Course

Before a trainee may be admitted as a solicitor, the compulsory Professional Skills Course must be undertaken. The cost of this course is borne by your employer. This can either be done by fast track in a few weeks or over two years. In most cases, your employer will determine the way in which you take the course.

On this course, you will cover Advocacy and Oral Communication, Financial Awareness and Business Accounts, Ethics and Client Responsibilities. It is generally felt that trainees get more out of these topics once they have some experience of work under their belt.

Pupillages

It is worth noting that a trainee barrister has to do one year for his or her apprenticeship rather than two, like a trainee solicitor. The year is divided into two sets of six months, often referred to as 'sixes'. It is possible to do both in the same chambers, but it is more usual to do each six in a different set. You will be assigned to a particular person, who is called your Pupil Master. They will oversee your time at that set of chambers but you may be assigned by them to shadow others in the set.

During the first six, you will find yourself observing and helping your Pupil Master to prepare cases. After your first six you will receive a certificate, which means you can take on your own work. Amanda recalled how she couldn't wait to get stuck in, then how she was terrified when she had to do it!

Pupillages have become more flexible these days. You may also count work undertaken with a qualified solicitor in England and Wales, a qualified lawyer in an EU country, a professional person whose work is relevant to practice or a member of the Employed Bar, which is the term for those barristers who work for an employer rather than independently. You can also count marshalling for a judge, which I referred to earlier in relation to work experience. It is also possible to work in the European Commission in one of the legal departments. This is known as a 'stage'. The Inns of Court arrange for four students each year to work for five months in Brussels. You can also work in London with the office of the European Commission. If you are particularly interested in Housing and Family Law, you may look into doing one of your sixes at a local authority. You could also consider the Crown Prosecution Service (CPS). The Bar Council will be able to tell you what is acceptable for your pupillage.

You will have to complete three compulsory courses, in Advocacy, Advice to Counsel and Accounts. The Inns of Court provide training courses for these. Amanda spent a weekend away at a conference centre for her Advocacy course. She found it hard work, but helpful. It involved videoed presentations and talks by senior practitioners. Each Inn will have its own way of conducting these courses. It might influence your choice of Inns at the outset if you like the way they cover these compulsory topics.

How do I apply?

You will need to look at what areas interest you. Amanda recommends a general common law set, covering Criminal, Family,

Personal Injury, Landlord and Tenant, Employment and Medical Negligence. She felt it was better to start with a broad base and specialize later. You, however, may prefer to focus on one area, such as a solely Criminal or Commercial set. Louise advised against picking chambers that cover subjects that you do not enjoy. However, you may not be in a position to be fussy!

Pankaj emphasizes the importance of proper research at this stage. You will need to know how much work there is at the bottom end of the practice, as that is where you will be starting. It is no good if there is a lot of work for the silks (the senior barristers), but not much for the juniors. You should also look ahead to see what chance there is of being taken on as a tenant. Pankaj rang up all the people with whom he had established contact, and sought their advice. Using such people as a sounding board will help you make the right choice.

The Chambers and Pupillages Award Handbook, which I mentioned in relation to work experience, will provide you with a significant amount of information. Pupillages may be either funded or unfunded. Some chambers will pay you an award as a pupil, to help meet your expenses until you start earning money. If, during a funded pupillage, you are going to receive less than £2,000, the Bar Council's interest-free loan scheme may assist you. A commercial pupillage may pay as much as £20,000 per annum or more. As you might expect, there is fierce competition for these places. Such firms look for academic excellence as a basic requirement. Some sets provide an income guarantee, so that you don't starve! This means that your income will not fall below a certain amount.

> **Tip:** Make sure you comply with the basic requirements for each chambers as set out in the *Handbook*.

Louise commented that over half of the applications sent in to her chambers simply did not comply with the minimum requirements, such as sending in a stamped addressed envelope and a handwritten covering letter. This meant an immediate 'no' as far as a pupillage was concerned, even though the student might have a lot going for him or her. When there is tough competition, anything that weeds people out is useful.

There is a Pupillage Fair every year, held at different venues, where chambers set up stalls. It is worth going along to chat to those running the stall and find out what their pupillage policy is. It is most unlikely that you would be offered a job at a Fair, but you might pick up some useful information.

A relatively new scheme has been the Pupillage Applications Clearing House (PACH). It works a bit like university clearing. It limits students to twelve applications, in the hope that they will pick those chambers to which they are really suited, rather than making blanket applications to every chambers in England and Wales. The timetable for applications is set in the spring each year. Students can contact the Education and Training Department of the Bar Council for further details.

Some chambers are outside the scheme, and you will have to apply to these separately. If you try to apply to a PACH chambers other than through the scheme, you will be unsuccessful. Chambers in the scheme are not allowed to make offers to non-PACH applicants until after the offer and acceptance date.

Pankaj found the interview time for pupillages stressful. Not only was he trying to cope with Bar School, but he was having to travel to interviews as well. He recalls one particular day when he attended five interviews, and covered hundreds of miles!

What is it really like?

Louise did an unfunded pupillage. She had to pay for her accommodation, but chambers paid for her travel. She also found that, generally, she did not have to pay for any food in chambers; the person with whom she was working picked up the bill. She found the first six difficult financially, until she could start taking on her own work. After that, about half-way through her second six, she was earning enough to keep herself and pay commission to the Clerk. (For more information on the role of a barrister's Clerk, see Chapter 5.) Louise practises mainly in Criminal Law. She feels it is important to ask how often you would be in court as a pupil because it was vital to start building up work; this is only possible with frequent court visits.

Amanda did a funded pupillage. She was paid a sum when she started, and again at Christmas during her first six. Her chambers had an income guarantee, so she knew she would be able to manage financially.

Pankaj was in court about three or four days each week. He was lucky enough to have the opportunity to appear before a High Court judge on a couple of occasions. He was also able, as was Amanda, to prosecute as an agent for the Crown Prosecution Service. This provided experience of the Magistrates' Court, where the work is quite different from that of the Crown Court. He felt that these experiences taught him how to cope with a large volume of paperwork and how to conduct a trial without a judge and jury. In the Magistrates' Court the Justices decide on questions of fact as well as law. As far as income was concerned, Pankaj found he could earn about £17,000 during the first six months of taking work in his own right.

You will have to consider taking on an accountant as you start to earn. This issue is dealt with in the Advice to Counsel course.

Will I need a wig and gown?

You will already be aware that barristers wear a black gown and a horsehair wig in the Crown Court and higher courts. Traditionally, these were used in order to provide anonymity for the advocate in court. They are not cheap, and you may prefer to borrow for a while. Amanda advises not rushing out to buy them straight away, until you can see what your circumstances are likely to be. She also suggests looking on the notice board at your Inn to see if there are any second-hand sets for sale.

What happens when it doesn't happen

Sometimes, despite your best efforts, things do not work out. The important point to remember is that it happens to most people at one stage or another as they go through life. It does not mean that you are a failure. Plenty of people have gone on to great things as a result of a perceived setback. It may mean that you end up in a situation that you would never have considered if everything had gone according to plan.

Tim was not sure which area of practice he wanted to go in for. He had not secured a Training Contract by the end of the LPC, and went to work for a local housing and advice centre. He had undertaken some work with the centre during the option stage of the LPC. He was dealing with all manner of queries and cases which arose in areas such as Landlord and Tenant Law, Housing Law, and homelessness. Although there were some salaried staff, Tim was involved largely on a voluntary basis. He then got a job working in the general administration office for his local Magistrates' Court. As a result, he is now considering training as a Court Clerk.

Rachel did a sandwich Law degree, which led to her spending her year out at a Magistrates' Court. She was initially very keen to qualify as a Court Clerk and do her Training Contract that way. However, she ended up working for a general practice with a high proportion of legally aided clients. She was taken on in a paralegal capacity and, having proved her worth, was offered a Training Contract. She has specialized in Family Law and, although she has found it tremendously hard work, with very long hours, the job satisfaction is ample reward. It was not at all what she set out to do. Rachel was able to apply for the maximum of 12 months' remission from her Training Contract as a result of the paralegal work she did.

There are many other ways of using the skills you have now acquired. You might consider working in local government, teaching or research. You could also look at the legal departments of large businesses. Some charities and other bodies may consider people with a legal background. Whatever you decide, the important thing is not to give up.

4

Admission as a solicitor

Once you have completed your Training Contract, you will be able to apply to the Law Society to be admitted to the Roll as a Solicitor of the Supreme Court. That is the fancy title for the process of qualifying. You will be invited to a ceremony at the Law Society, where you will be introduced to the Society's President and enjoy tea in splendid surroundings.

Private practice

Most solicitors work in private practice. When you think of a solicitor, you probably imagine him or her in the context of an office on your local high street. However, private practice can cover many different areas, some of which are specialized.

General practice

Greg works in a general practice in a thriving town in the north of England. There are four fee earners. He actually got the job because he wrote to the firm looking for a Training Contract. At that time they had no vacancies, but they kept his details on file. He was surprised when they wrote to him a year into his Training Contract offering him a position as he did not expect to hear from them again. Greg is now doing what he always imagined solicitors did. People come into the office and he undertakes their conveyancing, probate and general litigation, as well as the drawing up of their wills. They come in with a range of problems, some of which he hopes to be able to help with. He finds the job satisfaction is high, as people are delighted when the job is done. Greg has an excellent quality of life; he is able to balance his career with social activities, as the hours of work are not excessive.

Greg was actually an accountant by training but found that he was progressively more attracted by law. When he was negotiating with unsecured creditors in insolvencies, he found that he wanted to know what the legal boundaries were. One thing led to another and he made a decision, with a view to the long term, to change career. It could not be done overnight because he had to save up sufficient money to fund the various courses that were necessary. It was in fact another two or three years before he was able to embark on training for his new career. It was certainly not easy, as he was having to spend a significant amount of money with no prospect of a return until he secured his Training Contract.

James practises in Criminal Law in a medium-sized firm in the south of England. He originally thought about a career in Business Law, having chosen a degree suited to that, but found that he did not enjoy the work. He ended up doing Matrimonial work as part of a work placement after his degree, and was taken on by the firm to do such work, but has actually spent most of his time in the Criminal department. He particularly enjoys police-station work, when he is on call as the duty solicitor. He never knows what will be waiting when he gets a call out, and he often finds it quite an adrenalin rush! He also likes the fact that he has the chance to build up a relationship with clients.

Claire works in a small local practice in the south of England. She also specializes mainly in Criminal work. Much of her work is based in the Magistrates' Court. On some days, she is on duty at court, to represent people who have not seen a solicitor and who need immediate general legal advice about their case. As with police-station work, she has to be prepared for anything. You certainly have to be able to talk to people you have never met before and establish what they need to do. People in this situation are often very nervous. In a fairly small, rural court, there is also the need to build up a rapport with the magistrates who may frequently see you representing clients.

Commercial practice

Danielle works in what may be described as a small niche commercial practice in Leeds, now the most important legal centre in England after London, and growing quickly. Her Training Contract in the Midlands led to her becoming involved in work in a commercial setting. The firm she was with steered her towards that area, so that her career evolved in that direction rather than taking that route as the result of a deliberate choice.

Although Danielle's is a specialist firm, it covers a broad range of areas, including Employment Law, Insolvency and contractual disputes. As a litigator, Danielle has found that there are fewer women in the commercial field. I wondered how the contact with clients differed from the contact experienced in a general practice. Danielle indicated that in some cases she is dealing with the directors and owners of companies, and not seeing the individuals affected by the litigation; she feels that it is important to remember that there are often jobs at stake. This spurs her on to achieve the 'right' result. At the same time, she stressed to me that she has to draw a fine line between being motivated by those behind the scenes and getting too emotionally involved. The fact that she does not meet those being affected means that, in reality, the job does not become too personal.

Danielle's view is that it is important to work hard and play hard as a lawyer. Combining the two promotes a balance that has a positive effect on a lawyer's working life, so it is essential that a person coming into the profession finds a place that enables them to do this.

Shilpen also chose to work in a commercial field. His family had a background in business and he liked the 'edge' that this line of work provided. During his Training Contract he got the opportunity to deal with Commercial and Civil clients and sometimes with so-called 'white collar' Criminal clients, that is to say, those involved in fraud. At the time when he qualified, the job being offered was weighted towards Criminal Law, so he took the opportunity to move to a different part of the country and do Commercial litigation. On a typical day there will be correspondence to go through and letters to write. There might be affidavits (sworn statements) to draft and file. After that, there may be an amount of negotiation to conduct in order to try to settle cases. Shilpen finds that excellent interpersonal skills are essential.

Someone who is newly qualified, or has up to three years' post-qualification experience (PQE), could earn between £20,000 and £30,000 in a smaller specialized practice. You would be likely to earn more with the larger commercial companies, but you have to weigh up what is important to you. You might find that with a larger firm you have less individual responsibility and that you work more in teams.

Shilpen's advice to someone seeking a career in the legal profession is not to listen to people who are negative about prospects and the profession itself. There are enough obstacles in life, without being told that you cannot do something.

Magistrates' Courts Service

This is my own area. I have been in the service for four years and undertook my Training Contract while working. I was effectively training for the job at the same time as training to be a solicitor. My job title is Court Clerk, but actually 'Legal Advisor' would be more accurate. (Some Court Clerks now prefer this title.) It is a very small area for solicitors to practise in. At my Law Society tea, I was the only one from the Magistrates' Courts Service!

As the title suggests, I spend a large proportion of my time in court. I sit in court, usually in front of the magistrates, and manage the business of the day. That means looking at the list of cases for the particular court and deciding how and when to call the cases on. When the magistrates need to know the extent of their legal powers, they can turn to me for advice. People who come to court unrepresented by a solicitor or barrister rely on me to make sure that they have a fair hearing and that they understand the proceedings. It is very much a people-centred job, and the job-holder needs to be a good communicator.

The Magistrates' Court deals with a wide variety of work. Nearly all Criminal cases start and finish in the Magistrates' Court. A small percentage go up to the Crown Court, as the magistrates do not have power to hear them. These include offences such as murder and robbery, which start in the Magistrates' Court before proceeding upwards. (This may change in years to come.) By and large, the Criminal work is our bread and butter, and we deal with cases ranging from burglary to riding a bicycle without lights. There are also Family Proceedings courts, Youth courts, and private prosecutions brought by individuals or bodies such as the Health and Safety Executive. In addition, there is Liquor Licensing, which is the regulation of licences for public houses and social clubs in the area of the court. You never get two days the same. In the main, the work is stimulating and varied.

Aside from the court work I also have duties in servicing one of the magistrates' panel committees, which meet two or three times a year. I take the minutes for my panel and help the chairman organize the agenda and guest speakers. In addition, there are summonses to check, legal aid applications to process, general queries to answer and paperwork from the court.

During my Training Contract I was also being trained as a Court Clerk. I was able to take courts before I finished my Training Contract. This means not wasting any time and getting into the job very quickly. I rarely felt that I was an isolated individual who was just sitting by, unable to become involved, and within a short time I was very much part of the team.

It is not a job to take if you want to earn big money. It provides a steady income with salaries being set by reference to points on a nationally agreed scale. You are also likely to be offered a local government pension. A legally qualified clerk who has completed a Training Contract can start on over £20,000. A senior clerk could expect a salary of around £28,000.

One point to mention is that I do not handle clients' money in the same way that a solicitor in private practice does. As a result, I do not need to hold a practising certificate, which is a kind of insurance that solicitors must have when they represent clients. From a practical point of view, this means that, although I can sit on one side of the table in court and advise the magistrates, I may not cross to the other side and represent someone. This would not preclude me from obtaining a practising certificate, however, if I decided to go into private practice.

Crown Prosecution Service

This area, in common with the profession as a whole, has felt the effects of economic pressures in recent times. A few years ago there was a significant influx of lawyers, both solicitors and barristers, to the CPS, as the pay was good and the hours were reasonable. Another advantage was the lack of the usual overheads that have to be covered by a solicitor in private practice. As a result, the CPS recruitment situation is very tight at the moment, however, it is still a career option worth considering.

The CPS works in close consultation with the police in prosecuting Criminal cases. After someone has been arrested and charged with an offence, the police submit the file to the CPS, where it is reviewed by a lawyer. The lawyer decides whether charges are appropriate and assesses the strength of the evidence. You will spend a large proportion of your time in court, usually in the Magistrates', but sometimes on your own or with counsel at the Crown Court. The workload is varied. You can find yourself prosecuting a murder one minute and dealing with a defective tyre case the next.

The hours worked depend upon the court sittings, and you will also need to do a certain amount of preparation for the next day. You need to be able to think on your feet and to deal with all kinds of people. If you are prosecuting a trial, you will have to talk to any Crown witnesses and explain what is going to happen. This means being able to handle often nervous and distressed people in a sensitive and professional way.

There is a salary scale in the CPS, running from about £22,000 for a prosecutor starting out newly qualified to £40,000 plus for a very senior prosecutor.

Specialist prosecution

Claire works for the Environment Agency. She left school at 16 with eight O levels and went straight to work for her local city council. She spent eight years in the administrative office. She studied for an ONC (Ordinary National Certificate) and then an HNC (Higher National Certificate) in Business Studies and Public Administration.

At that stage, she decided to study Law. She gained a Law A level through night school, and followed this up with a part-time Law degree over four years. Half-way through her degree, she secured a job as a legal assistant with the National Rivers Authority, as it was then known.

Her employers paid for the rest of her degree and she was authorized to prosecute cases in the Magistrates' Court. This is quite common practice in such specialized areas, which also include the Health and Safety Executive and Trading Standards Department. Officers may be authorized to deal with straightforward cases in the Magistrates' Court without being qualified lawyers. It helps to keep the costs down and qualified lawyers may be brought in if the case warrants it.

Claire was fortunate in that the LPC was validated as a part-time course at the time when she needed to study it. She was credited with 12 months' work, which was remitted from her two-year Training Contract. This took into account the time that she had already spent at work as an authorized prosecutor. She spent six months in the conveyancing department, dealing with buying and selling land owned by the NRA. She was also sent out into private practice for six months to a large firm to complete her training. She studied the PSC by the fast track route and was offered a job as a solicitor with the new Environment Agency.

It took Claire 10 years to qualify, but what an achievement! Now, as a specialist litigator, Claire reviews case before they proceed to court. She deals with Environmental Law and this can cover anything from major river pollution to unlicensed fishing. Sometimes, a case may appear innocuous on the surface, but proves to be less than straightforward in reality. The hours she works depends on the court at which she is working. If the court runs late, she may have a long day.

A specialist prosecutor could earn £18,000 as a starting salary, rising on a scale to around £27,000.

Claire's advice is not to give up if you have decided what you really want to do. However, she says she always tried to keep a broad view, reminding herself that there were other jobs available if things did not work out.

The Armed Forces

According to its careers office, the British Army offers some openings for lawyers. If you are interested, you should contact your local area office (find their number in the telephone directory). Generally, it takes lawyers who are already qualified, and there is an upper age limit of 33 years. There may, however, be some limited forms of sponsorship available for training at university and postgraduate level. However, the onus is firmly on the individual to qualify and then apply for officer entry. Normal training requirements are waived for professionals such as doctors and lawyers who want to join the Army. Instead, a limited training programme is undertaken.

There is no specific need for solicitors in the Royal Navy, although it does have a very small number of naval barristers. The advice from the Navy's careers office to a budding lawyer who wants a career at sea is to go for officer entry as a graduate in the normal way. Apparently, it can be an excellent career, but there is no specific career structure as such for a lawyer.

Local Authority

Anna works for a local authority as a solicitor. She specializes in Family and Housing work. She came into the profession by the CPE route, having read French with Latin for her degree. She did some work experience involving child-care work while at university and this directed her towards a career in that area. She did her Training Contract at a large commercial firm, which confirmed her feeling that this was not the type of work she wanted to do. After qualifying, she joined a firm that specialized in Matrimonial work but found that, after about three and a half years, she was ready for a change. She spent some time travelling, and then went to work for a local authority.

There is a care caseload to manage in local authority work, as in other areas. This involves initiating care proceedings within a time framework. There are experts to instruct and case conferences to attend, as well as evidence to collate. Aside from care proceedings, there are Education Supervision Orders to undertake, and prosecutions for failing to ensure a child's attendance at school. On the housing side, you might be dealing with a claim concerning someone's right to buy council property. In addition, you might find yourself having to cover specialist areas on occasions, such as litigation concerning residential homes run by the local authority.

Clearly, a career in this sort of field can be emotionally demanding. You need to be able to stand back. You are likely to find yourself frequently viewed as the enemy and you must be able to cope with that. In addition, the public's perception of this sort of work is not always favourable. On the other hand, this sort of work can be very rewarding, especially when you achieve a result that you know is right for those concerned.

On the positive side, the hours are flexible, and the work is varied and interesting. You could expect to earn in the region of £22,000 to £25,000.

5

Life at the Bar

Once you have been called to the Bar, you will become a member of a very prestigious profession, of which you will have some experience by this time. The majority of barristers work independently, on a self-employed basis, through sets of 'chambers'; the remainder work at what is called the 'Employed Bar'.

Working in chambers

You will hear the word 'chambers' used often in connection with barristers, but what are they? When barristers are self-employed, they usually work in groups – although one barrister may work on his or her own – from a suite of rooms. The term 'chambers' can refer to the rooms themselves, in a physical sense, but also to the collective organization of the barristers.

Once they are effectively established in chambers, barristers are able to advertise for work. A set of chambers may put out a glossy brochure indicating what sort of work they take on. (It is worth noting that a barrister may never be employed by an organization and also operate independently from chambers. This is to protect the independence of the Bar.)

Barristers in chambers are not only working for the collective good of the chambers, but also for their own independent living. This obviously requires a balancing act on the part of the individual, in respect of their own needs and those of their colleagues. More difficult and complex cases may require teamwork for consultation on research and strategy. Sometimes, more than one barrister is instructed on a case. The senior barrister 'leads' the junior one.

Barristers obtain work in the form of 'briefs' through chambers, but may prepare and carry out the work on an individual basis. The brief is the set of papers put together by the solicitor for the barrister, containing all the information he or she will need in preparation for the case – in other words, they are designed to 'brief' the barrister. Briefs are recognizable by the pink tape in which they are tied. 'Brief' is also a nickname for a barrister.

The chambers will contain a library and there will be clerical and support staff. The cost of these is divided in some agreed way between the members of the chambers. Within chambers there will also be a hierarchy of seniority and experience, from the Head of Chambers down to the pupil barristers.

Finding a tenancy

A 'tenancy' is the term used when a qualified barrister is invited to join a set of chambers as a permanent member. She or he is then referred to as a 'tenant'.

To say that the situation is tight at present would be an understatement. It is not uncommon for people to undertake third and fourth sixes – the six-month period of apprenticeship before becoming a fully fledged barrister – in terms of pupillage, while two sets of six is the normal requirement. There is even a phenomenon known as 'squatting', in which people who are not pupils or tenants are allowed by the goodwill of certain chambers to carry on practising.

The advice being offered from those already in, is mostly common sense. Build up a good relationship with everyone in chambers, and not just with your Pupil Master. Use opportunities to interact with the other barristers in chambers. Offer to do work rather than waiting to be asked. Never say 'no' to work put your way, or say that you are too busy. As a pupil, it is likely that you will be assessed for a tenancy while you are doing your pupillage. Never make the mistake of behaving as though you are a tenant, even if you are working in what appears to be a very relaxed set. This does not go down well at all. It only takes a rumour to blow your chances. It is not just about how good you are as a lawyer; the chambers must have confidence in you as a person too.

Pankaj felt it was very important to use much care when selecting a set of chambers for pupillage. In his view, you need to think ahead, in order to assess whether or not the set is likely to have a vacancy for a tenancy at the end. He sought advice from a variety of contacts and colleagues before making his choice. He suggests that the Inns of Court might be a useful source of information on this point. You need to know that there will be work available for you as a pupil at the bottom end of the ladder, so that you can demonstrate an ability to make a living. If there is only work for the more senior members of chambers, then you are going to struggle. It is therefore important that the chambers should attract work on a wide range of cases in the areas in which it practises.

How do you get paid?

This is an interesting part of being a barrister. Your fee, or the money that you charge, is treated as an 'honorarium' – a voluntary fee paid to a professional person for their services. As such, if the fee is not paid promptly, you are not able to claim interest on it, nor are you able to sue if it is not paid at all. This means, in reality, that barristers are dependent upon others paying their fees on time. In most cases, the money will be owed to the barrister by a solicitor! If the fee is not paid, then it is the solicitor who has to sue the debtor for the money on the barrister's behalf. As a barrister, you will definitely need to have a good relationship with your bank manager! Sometimes it can take years to receive fees. You may think that I am exaggerating, but I am not. One prize example of this difficulty was a fee note for advice on damages dated 26 October 1972 that was not paid until 18 February 1994!

Once you become a tenant, some of your earnings will go towards the running costs of chambers. There will also be income tax and professional fees to cover. It is important to have an accountant to deal with this side of the job, so that you can concentrate on earning the money.

As far as earnings are concerned, barristers can make very good money, but not necessarily as much as the tabloid press would have us believe.

What does a barrister's Clerk do?

The job of the barrister's Clerk is enormously skilled. The Clerk might not have any formal qualifications, but he or she is one of the most important people in chambers. It is vital to your success in chambers to make an effort to get on with the Clerk. Clerks have usually been in their job a long time and know the system far better than you. They bring the work in from the solicitors and give the briefs to the various tenants. If you are going to get enough work, and get work of the type that you enjoy, you are going to have to look after your Clerk. Clerks may be salaried or earn a percentage of chambers income, or both. Even as a pupil, you may find that you start paying a percentage to the Clerk as soon as you take on work in your own right.

The Clerk in chambers has a difficult task in assigning work. It is important that the job is done well so that solicitors keep instructing the chambers. Some briefs come into chambers marked for a particular barrister. Others may not be assigned, in which case the Clerk has to make a decision. He or she cannot necessarily employ the 'cab rank' rule – that is, passing it to whoever is next in line – when giving out work. He must assign it to the best person for the job. This can be tricky when there is more than one barrister doing work of the same nature. It will quickly become obvious who is getting the work and, therefore, who is considered to be the most competent.

What sort of work is available?

The range of work you do will depend on what sort of chambers you choose. If you go for a general set, they are likely to cover most areas of legal practice. This is more likely to be the case in the sets outside London. You might find yourself having to cover a very broad range of subjects. This could include Criminal, Family, Contract, Commercial, Landlord and Tenant, Defamation and Agricultural Law. On the other hand, in London you may find sets that specialize in just two or three of these fields.

Louise practises mainly in Criminal Law but also does some Immigration Law and industrial tribunals. She prosecutes and defends, but not at the same time! You have to get used to being flexible as far as that aspect is concerned. The hours can be long; many do not leave chambers before 7.30pm on an average day, and there will often be work to do at home for the rest of the evening.

Whether you are based inside or outside London, you are likely to find that frequent travel is necessary. You might have a brief in one place first thing in the morning, followed by a journey to another court later the same morning, and then on somewhere else during the afternoon. After all the travelling there may be a conference with solicitor and client back at chambers later that same afternoon. When the working day has finished, the preparation for the next day starts. There is no getting away from the hard work, but one of the bonuses of a career of this sort is that you will rarely be bored!

Work in court

A large proportion of the barrister's time is, of course, spent in court. As far as work at the Crown Court is concerned, this will involve more serious Criminal cases. There may be bail applications to make before one of the judges in his chambers (the room he retires to when he is not in the courtroom). That tends to take place before the business of the day. You will meet up with your instructing solicitor, who may sit behind you during the proceedings, to assist with any details that arise. Your main role is to provide your client with the specialist advocacy he or she needs in order to present the case.

You will get used to the formalities of court, including certain turns of phrase. For example, you refer to a fellow barrister as 'my learned friend', and the judge is always referred to as 'Your Honour'. You may have to conduct a trial before a jury. If you appear in the Magistrates' Court, the proceedings are conducted in a less formal way. You do not have to wear a wig and gown, for example. There is no jury in the court, and the magistrates decide on matters of fact and law.

The Employed Bar

There are many other jobs available if you qualify as a barrister but decide to opt for being employed rather than taking work independently. For example, you might consider working in the public sector, either in a local authority or for the Magistrates' Courts Service. They recruit both qualified solicitors and barristers to work as legal advisers. You could also look at a career in the Crown Prosecution Service. As a practising, self-employed barrister it is possible to be instructed to do agency prosecutions for the CPS. As an employed barrister you could work for them full-time on a salaried basis.

The Navy recruits a very limited number of barristers for work at sea and there are also opportunities for lawyers in the army (see Chapter 4).

There are also jobs within the legal departments of companies. You could also look at organizations such as the Health and Safety Executive and HM Customs and Excise. They have legal departments that investigate offences and prepare prosecutions. Although some inspectors who are not legally qualified are authorized to prosecute cases, both institutions still require a number of lawyers.

6

Summary

General points

- Unless you are absolutely sure from the start, investigate both branches of the profession.
- Do some work experience.
- Plan ahead well in advance of the next stage.
- Stick to traditional subjects for GCSE and A levels.
- Unless you have clear advice to the contrary, don't dabble in studying Law before degree level.

Barristers

1. Law degree covering the Seven Foundations of Legal Knowledge, or non-Law degree and Common Professional Examination.
2. Join an Inn of Court.
3. Bar Vocational Course (12 months).
4. Complete 12 qualifying units.
5. Called to the Bar.
6. Pupillage (12 months).
7. Tenancy.

Minimum time for qualifying as a barrister is five years.

Solicitors

1. Law degree covering the Seven Foundations of Legal Knowledge, or non-Law degree and Common Professional Examination or non-degree route (ILEX).
2. Student membership of Law Society.
3. Legal Practice Course (12 months).
4. Training Contract (two years) including Professional Skills Course.
5. Admission as a solicitor.

Minimum time for qualifying as a solicitor is six years.

How much is it going to cost me?

I cannot quantify the cost in terms of blood, sweat and tears, but I can give you a general idea of the finances!

Barristers

After your degree, you will have to pay for:

- Common Professional Examination (non-Law graduates): £2,300–4,500 (depending on where you study).
- Certificate of Completion of the Academic Stage: £50
- Entrance fee to Inn: £85.
- Cost of dining: £9.50 per dinner for student members (12 units to be completed).
- Bar Vocational Course: £6,500.
- Costs of keeping yourself during pupillage (six months minimum, until you can start taking work).
- Wig and gown: £550.
- Call fee: £80.

This does not take into account any books you will need to buy along the way.

Solicitors

After your degree you will have to pay for:

- Common Professional Examination (non-Law graduates): £2,300–4,500 (depending on where you study).
- Certificate of Completion of the Academic Stage: £50.
- Student membership of the Law Society: £70.
- Legal Practice Course: £5,000–6,500 (depending on where you study).
- Costs of keeping yourself during your Training Contract, in relation to how much you are paid (two years).
- Admission fee: £80.

Again, this does not take into account any books you will need to buy along the way.

Where can I obtain funding?

There are limited sources of funding available. If there is any way you can avoid high levels of debt, take advantage of it. However, sometimes you may have to accept that there is no choice if you are going to pursue your chosen career.

The whole funding issue has recently been under consideration by the Law Society and the Bar Council. The Trainee Solicitors Group in particular has been campaigning with some success to open up avenues of funding for those going into that branch of the profession. Below is an outline of some of the options available. If you want more detailed information, you should contact the Bar Council, the Law Society and the individual sources concerned.

Trainee solicitors and barristers

Local Authority grants
These are very scarce at this level. It depends on where you live. Some authorities have so many students going on to higher education that

the money is prioritized for those doing first degrees, leaving none for postgraduate studies. Although training to be a solicitor or barrister ought to be seen as studying for a career rather than as postgraduate study, this is not the case. If you are very lucky, your local authority may be in a position to consider postgraduate applications. Any awards made will be on a discretionary basis. You will need to investigate and find out how your local authority prefers you to apply.

Bank loans

Some of the high-street banks have special rates for those pursuing a legal career. National Westminster Bank has teamed up with the Trainee Solicitors Group in a scheme with special rates for LPC students who have secured a Training Contract. The HSBC (formerly Midland Bank) offers a Postgraduate Studies Loan. Barclays Bank offers a Professional Studies Loan scheme, and the Royal Bank of Scotland has a Law Student Loan Scheme. In each case contact your local branch as a starting point.

Career development loans

These are offered by the Department of Employment in conjunction with four banks: Barclays, the Clydesdale, the Co-operative and the Royal Bank of Scotland. They will pay up to 80 per cent of the course fees for the vocational courses, and also something towards living expenses if the course is full-time. The deal is that the person applying for the loan should be able to demonstrate that they intend to use the qualifications to obtain work either in the UK or the European Union. You cannot apply if you able to fund the courses from other sources. If, for example, you have sponsorship from an employer, then the door to this particular avenue of funding would be closed.

Hardship funds

Hardship funds, sometimes called access funds, exist to help gifted students with severe financial difficulties - it must be stressed that these relate to extreme hardship, and not to the normal 'hardship' that most students suffer! They are usually discretionary, and you need to find out how to apply from the college or institution itself.

Pupil barristers

Scholarships and awards from the Inns of Court
This applies only to those wanting to be barristers. The four Inns of Court offer a wide range of awards, which are designed to assist the student from the time he or she leaves university until the end of their pupillage. You should investigate what is on offer from each Inn when you are choosing which one to join. In each case there will be a particular member of staff who will be able to advise students on their particular needs.

Income guarantees and awards by chambers
Many sets now offer income guarantees to their pupils. This means that they are guaranteed a minimum income, regardless of how much they bring in during their pupillage. This minimum award is £3,000 per six months of pupillage. It at least ensures that the pupil does not starve! Some sets provide larger awards.

Bar Council loan
This is available for those students doing a pupillage who are getting less than £2,000 pa. An interest-free loan is available for up to £4,000.

Trainee solicitors

Sponsorship
Sponsorship is great, if you can get it! Some of the larger firms still provide financial assistance to those whom they have recruited. Usually, you have to have obtained a Training Contract with them before they will assist you with course fees. In most cases, you would expect to have to sign some sort of agreement to say that, once you start work, you will not leave the firm before a certain amount of time has elapsed. Naturally, they like to know that they are going to get some return on their investment.

Knowing that a particular firm provides this sort of sponsorship might persuade you to apply to join them. A starting point might be to try to obtain work experience with them. In any event, competition for sponsorship will be fierce!

Law Society Bursary Scheme

This refers to a group of funds put together from various sources. The money is limited, so strict criteria apply. The student needs to show that he or she is very talented, and genuinely unable to fund studies from other sources. A bursary application form may be obtained from the Law Society.

Ethnic minorities

There are a number of awards available for ethnic-minority students who are British citizens who want to qualify as solicitors. The Law Society might be the best first point of contact to find out what is available and who to contact.

Overseas students

The British Council should be able to assist with any queries regarding qualification in England and Wales for overseas students. Students with a work permit for the purpose of undertaking a Training Contract may apply to firms offering sponsorship for the vocational stages of qualification.

Glossary

Admission to the Roll: A term used to describe the occasion of qualification as a solicitor, when the new solicitor's name joins the list of qualified solicitors in England and Wales.

Advocate: Term that can refer to both solicitors and barristers as they represent a client in court and put forward his or her case.

The Bar: The collective body of barristers, in this case, in England and Wales.

Brief: A bundle of papers prepared by a solicitor for a barrister to provide him or her with all the information needed to take on a case. Recognizable by the pink tape in which it is tied. Can also be a nickname for a barrister.

BVC: Bar Vocational Course. The vocational year of training for a barrister. It used to be available only in London, but now other institutions around England and Wales are validated.

CACH: Centralized Applications and Clearing House. The system used to apply for a place on the Bar Vocational Course.

Call: The term used to describe the admission of someone who has qualified to the Bar of England and Wales. May only be done by the Inns of Court. Enables the qualified person to practise as an independent advocate after completing pupillage, or to work at the Employed Bar.

54 Glossary

Chambers: The suite of rooms used by a barrister or barristers who practise independently, from which they advertise for business.

CPE: Common Professional Examination. Covers the required legal subjects in one year. Particularly for graduates with non-Law degrees. Also for Law graduates whose degree does not exempt them from the CPE because it does not cover all the subjects. Can be studied part-time over two years.

Conference: A meeting between a barrister, the client and the instructing solicitor.

Dining in: The practice of dining at the Inns of Court before being called to the Bar. Twelve qualifying units must be completed; dining is a part of this, but other activities such as lectures and weekend residentials are also available.

Inns of Court: The ancient societies to which barristers must belong before they are called to the Bar. There are four: Gray's Inn, Inner Temple, Middle Temple and Lincoln's Inn, all in London.

LPC: Legal Practice Course. The vocational year of training for a solicitor. Also available part-time over two years.

Mooting: Like debating, a discussion of a hypothetical legal case, sometimes undertaken in a formal setting.

PACH: Pupillage Applications Clearing House. The system by which students apply for a pupillage. Limits the number of applications to 12.

PSC: Professional Skills Course, undertaken by trainee solicitors while they are under their Training Contract. Paid for by the employer, it covers areas that are only meaningful once some experience of practice has been attained.

Pupillage: A year's apprenticeship for barristers learning the profession.

Pupil Master: The more senior barrister who supervises the training of the pupil barrister.

Queen's Counsel (QC): An honorary rank of barristers who are highly experienced, and who deal with the most serious cases.

Silk: Another term for Queen's Counsel, deriving from his or her entitlement to wear a silk gown.

Tenancy: When a pupil barrister is invited to become a fully fledged member of chambers, he or she is referred to as a tenant.

Training Contract: The two-year apprenticeship of a trainee solicitor before Admission to the Roll. Used to be called Articles or Articles of Clerkship.

Want to know more?

Addresses

General

General Council of the Bar
Education and Training Department
2–3 Cursiter Street
London
EC4A 1NE
Telephone: 0171 440 4000

The Law Society
Ipsley Court
Redditch
Worcestershire
B98 0TD
Telephone: 01527 517141

A very important source of information is the national Careers Advice Network, which provides training information for solicitors and barristers in partnership with the Law Society and the Bar Council. If you contact the Law Society at the address above you will receive a superb pack outlining everything you need to know about the various courses, and when to apply. There is a list available of those organizations that are members of the Network on a regional basis, with details of the right person to contact in each case. Most careers advisers and Law Departments seem to be covered by the

Network, which means that it should be easy to gain access to an information pack.

CPE

For applications for the full-time course:
CPE Applications Board
PO Box 84
Guildford
Surrey
GU3 1YX
Telephone: 01483 451080

For applications for part-time courses, apply direct to the institution concerned.

Inns of Court

Gray's Inn
Education Department
8 South Square
London
WC1R 5EU
Telephone: 0171 405 8164

Inner Temple
Education and Training Department
Treasurer's Office
London
EC4Y 7HL
Telephone: 0171 797 8250

Lincoln's Inn
Students' Department
Treasury Office
London
WC2A 3TL
Telephone: 0171 405 0138

Middle Temple
Students' Department
Treasury Office
London
EC4Y 9AT
Telephone: 0171 427 4800

Specializations

The Association of Magistrates' Courts
79 New Cavendish Street
London
W1M 7RB
Telephone: 0171 436 8524

Government Legal Service
(A small number of Training Contracts are available in this area, details of which may be obtained from The Lawyers' Management Unit (address below).)

Institute of Legal Executives
Kempston Manor
Bedford
MK42 7AB
Telephone: 01234 841000

The Lawyers' Management Unit
Queen Anne's Chambers
28 Broadway
London
SW1H 9JS

LPC
Central Applications Board
PO Box 84
Guildford
Surrey
GU3 1YX
Telephone: 01483 301282

The Staff Management Unit
Crown Prosecution Service
50 Ludgate Hill
London
EC4M 7GG
Telephone: 0171 273 8357

Other groups

Trainee Solicitors Group
The Law Society
113 Chancery Lane
London
WC2A 1PL
Telephone: 0171 320 5794

Young Barristers Committee
The General Council of the Bar
3 Bedford Row
London
WC1R 4BD
Telephone: 0171 242 0082

Publications

Chambers and Partners Directory of the Legal Profession (Chambers and Partners Publishing)
Chambers and Pupillages Award Handbook (Bar Council)
Pritchard, John, *The Legal 500* (Legalease)
Solicitors' and Barristers' National Directory (Law Society)

Websites

Bar Council: http://www.barcouncil.org.uk
Law Society: http://www.lawsociety.org.uk